2008 中国汽车工业年鉴

CHINA AUTOMOTIVE INDUSTRY YEARBOOK

2008年版

CHINA AUTO 中国汽车

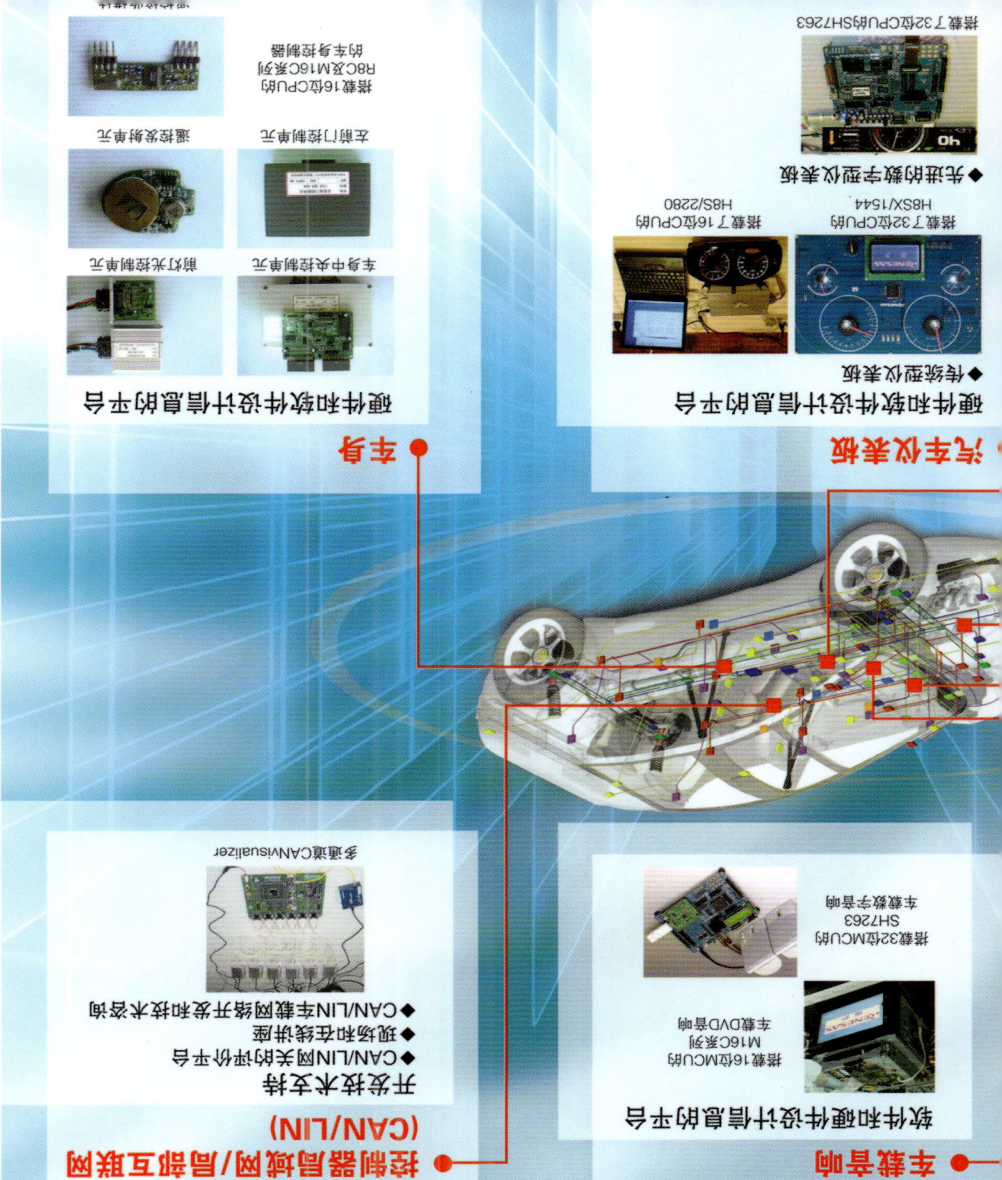

中国最美的城区之一
ONE OF THE MOST BEAUTIFUL URBAN DISTRICTS IN CHINA

序

信步在什刹海水岸,碧波荡漾,垂柳依依,清澈的湖水、幽深的街巷和古老的建筑,使我对什刹海的这片水域和这里的历史文物保护区,有着深深的感情。

元朝,依托这一片水域,在东岸确定了都城建设的中轴线。什刹海成为元大都城市规划的几何原点,是元、明、清三代城市规划和水系的核心。历经数百年的发展,什刹海积淀了上至皇族、士大夫,下至普通百姓的深厚的、多元的文化。同时,它又是现代人群的栖息地,传承下来的古老文明和生机勃勃的当代文化在此融合,让什刹海成为了展示老北京历史、文化的独特景观和典型载体,也是北京的一张亮丽名片。

什刹海是兼容并包、多元统一的,融合是什刹海的文化本质。什刹海的丰富性来源于各个民族的融合、皇家气象与百姓风俗的融合、人与自然的融合、宗教与世俗的融合。同时,什刹海又是"开放"的,海纳百川。作为元代漕运的起点,南来北往的货物运输,各国人员的来往交流,极大地丰富了京城的物品文化元素,也丰富了什刹海的文化内涵。今天的什刹海更是一片开放的区域,湖光山色,人影衣香,已成为北京对外开放、展示北京文化底蕴的重要场所和窗口。什刹海也是和谐、和睦的。这里庭院深深,胡同蜿蜒,各种人群和谐相处、平和宜居。

什刹海是古都之源、文化之源,很多京华烟云在什刹海上空凝聚、缭绕,给人们带来很多追忆、很多思索、很多怀念。《中国最美的城区之———北京什刹海》,邀您共赏什刹海的美景、回味什刹海的古韵、品味什刹海的民俗、悦览什刹海的新装,细细感受什刹海独具特色的文化。

Preface

Strolling around Shichahai area, you will be greatly enchanted by her beauty as willows drooping gracefully in the gentle breeze, numerous ripples shimmering against sunlight, long and quiet Hutongs full of stories and magnificent imperial mansions awaiting your exploration. You are bound to fall in love with Shichahai, an area rich in history and culture resources.

In Yuan Dynasty, the central axle of the imperial city ran along the east bank of Shichahai water area. When Dadu City of Yuan Dynasty was under construction, Shichahai area was chosen as the geometric center and ever since then was the central point for city and water systems planning through Ming, and Qing dynasties. Several hundred years of development has endowed Shichahai with diverse culture elements in which royal magnificence, literary romance and simplicity of the commons integrated perfectly. Nowadays, modern culture merges perfectly with ancient civilization, which makes Shichahai a unique tourist destination and an eye-catching showcase from which in-depth knowledge about Beijing's culture heritage can be gained and it's age-long history can be explored.

Shichahai embodies diverse features which are in great harmony with each other since fusion is at root of everything. The diversity of Shichahai originates from the harmony it enjoys. In this area, various ethnic minority groups co-exitst peacefully. When admiring royal magnificence, you can also have a glimpse into folk custom. And it's no surprise that in this area, you will find quite a lot religious sites dotted among residential estates. In this area, daily lifes runs on peacefully and everything is in great harmony.

"Opening up to the outside world" has been the main theme that goes through the long history of Shichahai. In Yuan Dynasty, Shichahai functioned as the starting point of canal transportation. With cargo ships traveling between the north and the south and frequent international communication conducted with various countries, commerce and culture development of the capital city were greatly advanced. Nowadays, Shichahai is more of an open area. With its beautiful sceneries and booming tourist industry, Shichahai has become an important platform for Beijing to demonstrate its open-up policy and achievements as well as its rich cultural heritage.

Age-old capital city and its culture are both originated from Shichahai area. It's here that stories and memories are glittering. So join us in this comprehensive tour and start experiencing Shichahai — one of the most beautiful urban districts in China, which will sure bring you great fun. Great sceneries, culture relics, local folk customs and modern elements are all waiting for your exploration.

Fuhua

什刹海古风新韵

京华胜地什刹海

朴初题

目录 Contents

第一篇	赏·美景如画	Section I　Enjoying Great Sceneries	1
	第一章：四季风光异	Chapter I　Beautiful Sceneries Around Four Seasons	3
	第二章：胜地佳景多	Chapter II　Great Scenic Spots and Interesting Places	13
第二篇	忆·古韵流长	Section II　Reminiscence over Charming Antiquities	25
	第一章：遗迹屹千秋	Chapter I　Age-old Relics	27
	第二章：侯门府苑深	Chapter II　Grand Mansions and Gardens of the Nobles	33
	第三章：故居访名士	Chapter III　Visiting Former Residences of Celebrities	45
	第四章：宝刹香火盛	Chapter IV　Religious Sites	63
	第五章：古桥倚夕阳	Chapter V　Ancient Bridges in Sunset	71
第三篇	品·京味民风	Section III　Hunting for Typical Beijing Features	75
	第一章：胡同意味长	Chapter I　Hutongs and Theirs Stories	77
	第二章：百姓享盛世	Chapter II　Daily Life in a Prosperous Age	87
	第三章：美食风味浓	Chapter III　Gourmand's Delight	95
	第四章：缤纷手工艺	Chapter IV　Colorful Handicrafts	101
第四篇	悦·新装多姿	Section IV　Face-Lift for More Fun	107
	第一章：旅游事业兴	Chapter I　Booming Tourist Industry	109
	第二章：休闲新风尚	Chapter II　Leisure Trends	115
	第三章：旧迹换新颜	Chapter III　Renovation Efforts	121
	第四章：保护与传承	Chapter IV　Preservation and Inheritance	131
后记		Postscript	

贵

美景如画

Enjoying Great Sceneries

壹 四季风光异
Beautiful Sceneries Around Four Seasons

贰 胜地佳景多
Great Scenic Spots and Interesting Places

能被誉为"中国最美的城区"之一，什刹海自有其让人倾情之处。亭台楼榭妩妍，云水百态生。什刹海的美，美的自然，美的灵秀。漫步临水岸边，无论雕梁画栋，还是流水落花，都别有韵致。沉醉藕花深处，你会发现，什刹海不仅最美，而且最多情。

As one of "the most beautiful urban districts in China", Shichahai sure has its special appeal. Pavilions and terraces dot everywhere and sceneries changes as water runs.
The beauty of Shichahai is so delicate, so graceful and natural that everything, whether it's richly ornamented building or running water with dropping flowers afloat, has a lasting appeal to strollers at bank. You will realize that Shichahai is not only beautiful but also affectionate when you are intoxicated with the sweet smell of lotus.

第壹章
Chapter I

四季风光异
Beautiful Sceneries Around Four Seasons

"西湖春、秦淮夏、洞庭秋",什刹海随着季节的脚步变换妆容。春花秋月,夏荷冬雪,每个季节都有看不完的景致,每个景致又有品不尽的意味。

In China, there are several most beautiful seasonal sceneries that you should never miss, which are "West Lake in spring, Qinhuai River in summer and Dongting Lake in autumn". In Shichahai, you can enjoy all these great views as season changes. Whether it's spring blossoms, autumn moon or summer lotus and winter snowscape, sceneries here always promise ever-lasting charm.

鼓楼里的铜壶滴漏,风光在一点一滴中悄然变化。
Clepsydra ins de the drum tower witnesses the slow change of the scenery.

老宅春潮涌
Old residences witness the coming of spring season

故园海棠开
Chinese crabapple blossoms inside old garden

三月花灿烂
Blossom in March

散漫杨花雪满堤
停船只在画廊西
东风底事催归急
不管狂夫碎似泥

——清·姜宸英

Spring 春

什刹海的春来得早，走得迟。又是一年芳草绿，细雨化做缕缕春。
随着春天的到来，柳色从鹅黄、淡绿，直到青葱一片。风摇柳浪，如同云烟氤氲的水墨长卷。风停水静之际，什刹海的水恰似一块晶莹剔透的翡翠。

The spring of Shichahai comes early and lingers for quite a long while. Grass greens every year. In misty rains, spring comes again.

As spring advances, willow will turn from light yellow to light green and then to jade green. As wind passing through, willow leaves billow like a scroll of misty inkwash painting. When wind ceases and tranquility is restored, the water of Shichahai resmebles a large piece of shining jade.

春意浓浓染长堤
Lake in spring

雨后空气新
After the summer storm

夏日蝉声唱
Cicadas chorusing in summer days

桥头清风爽
Bridge bathing in breeze

田田荷叶水濛濛
猎猎菰蒲剪剪风
欸乃蓬舟人不见
棹歌遥过翠林东

——明·高衍

Summer 夏

什刹海自古就是老北京避暑纳凉的好地方。

夏日午后，树上蝉声鸣唱，桥下水禽梳羽，自成一派水景野趣。待到夜幕低垂之时，清风习习，荷香沁人。此情此景，正如古人所吟："湖边不用关门睡，夜夜凉风香满家。"

Ever since ancient times, Shichahai area has been an ideal place for people to shun summer heat and enjoy cool airs.

In summer afternoons, cicadas are chorusing in the trees with water birds dressing feathers under the bridges, which forms a delightful waterscape. When night falls, there are sweet smells of lotus flowers in the passing breeze, which will remind you of the old poem "Living by the lakeside, you can sleep tight with doors open and gentle breeze will bring in sweet fragrance of the lotus flowers every night".

映日荷花别样红
Lotus flowers are prettier in the bright sunshine

立秋湖水寒
Lake in autumn

金色满乾坤
It's a golden world here

天凉好个秋
Cooling days in autumn

城西湖水剩清凉
古寺凌波树几行
十里芙蓉通太液
一方蒲荻宛潇湘

——明·袁中道

Autumn 秋

"萧萧梧叶送寒声"，一场秋雨，几片黄叶，转眼便是清秋时节。
秋阳中的石榴红了，庭院里的银杏黄了。秋叶宛如翩然起舞的凤蝶悠然而下，铺成条条五彩路，直至胡同的幽深处……

As the poem goes "Rustling leaves of phoenix trees fortell the approach of autumn". Leaves have fallen in autumn rains and crisp autumn days are coming.
In autumn sunshine, megranates are red while the leaves of the gingko trees in the courtyard have turned yellow. Autumn leaves fall like dancing butterflies and paths leading into the depth of Hutong have turned colorful…

秋色连波，层林尽染。
Color of autumn

一场大雪入隆冬
With a heavy snow befell the winter

寒鸭戏水添冬趣
Great fun watching ducks paddling in the cold water

湖心残雪待日出
The remaining snow in the middle of the lake awaits the sunrise

一片空明两岸苍
望来犹道是波光
看人踏向中流去
不借蒲帆与石梁

——明·汪逸

Winter 冬

"一片空明两岸苍"，什刹海尤显北国冬季之美。不管是雪花纷飞，还是冰雪初融，都独具情致。

时值大雪，一波寒潭，两岸苍茫，尽飘鹅毛；雪后初霁，银装素裹，凌花闪烁。时光在此凝固，定格在琼楼玉树的季节。

As the poem goes "both sides of the lake enjoy great serenity", winter in Shichahai exemplifies the beauty of north China. Snowflake-dancing and snow-melting views are equally appealing.

When it snows heavily, everything is covered in whiteness and your sight view will be blurred. When days clear up afterwards, everything is shining with ice-coating. Time seems standstill here in winter.

窗含千秋雪,门泊几艘船。
Enjoying snowscape from the window with a few boats mooring at the bank

第贰章
Chapter II

胜地佳景多
Great Scenic Spots and Interesting Places

什刹海水脉悠长，周边古迹众多，不同的位置，不同的角度，呈现出风格迥异的景致。历史上的三海美景曾被很多文人墨客吟咏，随着时间的推移，今日的什刹海又增添了许多具有时代特征的绝妙景色。

The waters of Shichahai have a very long history and the surrounding areas are abundant in historical relics. The lake view changes from different angles. The beauty of the lake has been praised time and again by lots of literators in the history. Today, you can also enjoy wonderful scenic spots of contemporary features while touring Shichahai area.

凭栏观荷

"一曲池台半畹花",什刹海因水而多情,水因荷花而更显灵性。

Appreciating Lotus Flowers by Handrails

As poem goes "pavilions stand by the bend of pool, half of which is covered by flowers". It is the water that makes Shichahai so affectionate and it is the lotus flower that makes water more vivacious.

前海晨曦
昨夜春雷阵阵,雨后天光如洗,前海美景在湿漉漉的水气中展开画卷。

Lake at Dawn
Last night the spring thunder rumbled and this morning the sky is blue. The beauty of the Qianhai Lake unfolds in the mist.

金锭春晓
金锭桥畔,春色染碧波;古庙斜树,对影两婆娑。

Spring Morning at Jinding Bridge
By the Jinding Bridge, the spring is mirrored in the green water. The shadows of the ancient temple and the inclined trees spread gracefully over the lake surface.

烟波柳渡
"半池鸭绿水,几阵柳丝风",位于后海北沿的"烟波柳渡"有着诗一般的意境。

Willow Ferry Blurred in Mist
"Wild ducks are playing in the clear water while breeze is gently caressing willows leaves." This poetic scene can be enjoyed at Houhai Beiyan.

望海夕照

风云俱净,湖水澄澈,夕阳下的望海楼流光溢彩,巍然耸立。水波中的倒影,若即若离,恍若海市蜃楼。

Sunset View at Wanghai Tower

When the wind stops blowing, clouds stand still and water restores its tranquility. Wanghai Tower is a shining object in the twilight, which constitute an appealing sight with its reflection in the water.

寒潭映雪
雪后的湖面，万籁俱静，空灵悠远。所有的喧嚣都在雪中沉寂，用宁静和寒冷勾画一幅冬日雪景图。
Snowscape over Winter Lake
Tranquility reigns over the surface of the lake after a snow. All hustle and bustle die away in this white world.

碧水桃花

"盈盈荷瓣风前落,片片桃花雨后娇"。桃花盛开的季节,正是春水盛涨的月份,也是什刹海最美的时候。

Peach Blossoms at Lakeside

Shichanai is in her prime beauty when spring comes. In this season, peaches are in full blossom and spring tides are high.

浮云万里

浮云常涨常消，时光千年一瞬。眼前云卷云舒，随风涌动；胸中心潮澎湃，久久不息。

Lake View at Sunset
Time flies. Seasons change quietly in a blink of eyes.

霞光潋影

日落前的苍穹,晚霞如火,万道金光闪耀天际,把整个视野渲染得瑰丽壮美。

Sunset Over the Lake

In the glorious glow of the twilight, the sky seems to be in fire. What a magnificent sight it is!

冰湖初泮

"八九河开,九九燕来"。乍暖还寒时,后海的冰面一天比一天薄,随着暖风渐进,融成一湾春水。

Ice Melting Over the Lake

A popular proverb holds that "during the eighth nine-day period after Dongzhi (i.e. 63 days after the winter solstice or midwinter. According to Chinese lunar calendar, the first nine-day period after the midwinter is "First Nine"), the river ice starts to melt, and during the ninth nine-day period, swallows return from the south" In early spring, ice over Houhai Lake starts melting and bit by bit, ice melts away and the lake comes back to live.

橹声唱晚

夕阳下摇橹，有别样的味道。一抹晚霞映在水上，由远及近，只只小船泛起长长的涟漪，在洒满金辉的水面上悠然划过。

Boats Sculling at Twilight

Sculling in the sunset brings a special experience. In the twilight, little boats drift in leisure on the golden surface of the lake and leave long ripples in their wake.

忆

古韵流长
Reminiscence over Charming Antiquities

数百年的什刹海源远流长，王府、故居、寺庙星罗棋布，熠熠生辉。这些遗迹有的保存完整，有的正在修复，有的已然消失，然而都在以各种各样的方式见证历史，见证逝去的跌宕岁月。

The history of Shichahai could be traced back to hundreds of years ago and in this area, mansions of princes, former residences of celebrities and temples distribute like shining stars in the sky. Some of these relics are still well preserved and intact, some are in repair and others are nowhere to be found. All these relics have witnessed the passing history in their own days.

壹 遗迹屹千秋 Age-old Relics
贰 侯门府苑深 Grand Mansions and Gardens of the Nobles
叁 故居访名士 Visiting Former Residences of Celebrities
肆 宝刹香火盛 Religious Sites
伍 古桥倚夕阳 Ancient Bridges in Sunset

第壹章
Chapter I

遗迹屹千秋
Age-old Relics

在漫长的历史发展中,什刹海地区留下了很多具有特殊作用的建筑,它们或是拱卫皇宫,或是鸣报时间。虽然历经数百年洗礼,在现代城市建筑的丛林之中,人们依然可见这些雄伟建筑的身影……

In the development of local history, many buildings of special function have been left in the district of Shichahai. They either serve as the guard of the royal palaces or the time announcing center for the whole city. Although hundreds of years has passed, people can still find these majestic buildings among the forests of modern architectures.

北京城中轴线
全世界最长,也是最伟大的南北中轴线穿过全城,北京独有的壮美秩序就由这条中轴的建立而产生。

—— 梁思成

The Central Axle of Beijing City
The longest and greatest north-to-south axle of the world runs through the whole city. The establishment of this central axle gave birth to the unique and magnificent order of Beijing city.

—— Liang Sicheng

钟鼓楼

位于北京城中轴线的北端。始建于元至元九年（1272），明永乐十八年（1420）在现址重建，是元、明、清时期北京全城报时的中心。

Bell and Drum Tower

It is located at the north end of the central axle of Beijing city. Originally built in the ninth year of Zhiyuan Period of Yuan Dynasty (A.D. 1272) and rebuilt in the eighteenth year of Yongle Period in Ming Dynasty (A.D.1420), this tower served as the time announcing center for the whole Beijing city in Yuan, Ming and Qing periods.

德胜门箭楼

位于西城北二环路（什刹海地区北部）北侧，始建于明正统四年（1439），是明清时期北京内城保存至今的两座箭楼之一。

Archery Tower of Desheng Gate

It's located in Xicheng District and on the north side of the north part of the 2nd Ring Road (the north part of Shichahai district). The construction was launched in the 4th year of Zhengtong Period of Ming Dynasty (A.D. 1439). This archery is one of the two existent archery towers from Ming and Qing dynasties.

第贰章
Chapter II

侯门府苑深
Grand Mansions and Gardens of the Nobles

三潭碧水、岸柳轻盈。什刹海得天独厚的地理位置和自然环境，引得昔日众多皇族重臣在此修府建苑。由于宅主人大都出身显赫，往往在建筑府邸上投入大量心血，一面购置名贵山石竹木，一面网罗大江南北的能工巧匠，其精湛程度，令人叹为观止。

Due to the advantageous geological location and natural environment of Shichahai, lots of senior officials and royal family members had their mansions built here in the past. Great effort had been taken and the exquisiteness of the craftsmanship has won great acclaim.

恭王府

原为乾隆朝大学士和珅的宅邸。嘉庆四年（1799）赐予其弟永璘，称庆王府。咸丰二年（1852）赐予其弟奕䜣，改名为"恭亲王府"。它是至今北京清代王府中保存最完整的一个。

Prince Gong's Mansion

It used to be the homestead of Heshen who was a Grand-Scholar-Minister of the Qianlong period in Qing Dynasty. In the fourth year of Jiaqing Period (A.D. 1799), the residence was awarded to the emperor's brother Yonglinc with the name changed to Prince Qing's Mansion. In the second year of the Xianfeng Period, this mansion was awarded to another brother Yixin and the name changed to "Prince Gong's Mansion". This architecture is the best preserved one of all prince mansions from Qing Dynasty.

恭亲王奕䜣
Prince Gong Aisin-Gioro Yixin

恭王府花园

又名萃锦园，花园集江南园林与北方建筑格局为一体，又融入了西洋建筑特色，是中国古典园林中的瑰宝，位居清代王府花园之首。

The Garden of Prince Gong's Mansion

It is also called Cuijin Garden. The layout of the garden has combined both north China and south China architecture layout style and at the same time has integrated western architecture characteristics. Thus this garden has become a treasure among the traditional Chinese gardens and tops number one among gardens of prince mansions from Qing Dyasty.

游廊　Covered Corridor

妙香亭　Miaoxiang Pavilion

恭王府花园三绝之一"大戏楼"
Grand Opera Tower — One of the three unique relics of Prince Gong's Mansion

大宫门
The Formal Gate of the Mansion (the second gate)

载沣，清末摄政王，溥仪生父。
Zaifeng, Puyi's natural father and Prince Regent at the late years of Qing Dynasty

醇亲王府（北府）

位于后海北沿44号，原为康熙年间大学士明珠宅第。乾隆末年，将此宅赐其第十一子成亲王永瑆。光绪十四年（1888）改赐醇亲王奕譞，为"醇亲王新府"，又称"北府"。

Prince Chun's Mansion (North Mansion)

It is located at No. 44 of Houhai Beiyan. In the beginning it was the homestead of Mingzhu, the Grand-Scholar-Minister of Kangxi Period of Qing Dynasty. In the late years of Qianlong period, this residence was awarded to the emperor's eleventh brother Prince Cheng whose name is Yongxing. In the fourteenth year of Guangxu Period (A.D. 1888), it was awarded to Prince Chun whose name is Yixuan and the place became "New Mansion of Prince Chun" ever since. It is also called the North Mansion.

绣楼
Boudoir

寝殿
Resting Hall

王府大门
The Front Gate of the Mansion

绣楼 Boudoir

奕劻
Yikuang's Portrait

庆王府

庆王府位于定阜街3号，为清末庆亲王奕劻府第。奕劻是原庆亲王永璘的嗣孙，道光三十年(1850)袭辅国将军。咸丰元年(1851)奕劻迁至定阜大街原大学士琦善的宅第。光绪十年(1884)晋封庆郡王，按王府规制改建，始称"庆王府"。

Prince Qing's Mansion

Prince Qing's Mansion is at No.3 of Dingfu Street and it used to be the mansion of Prince Qing Yikuang at the late years of Qing Dynasty. Yikuang was the grandson and heir of Prince Qing Yongling. In the thirtieth year of Daoguang Period (A.D.1850), he succeeded the peerage and became State Ministrant General. And in the first year of Xianfeng Period (A.D. 1851), Yikuang moved to the residence of former Grand Scholar -Minister Qishan. In the tenth year of Guangxu Period (A.D. 1884), he was promoted to a higher level of nobility as Prefectural Monarch of Qing and the residence was rebuilt to meet the requirements for the new title. From then on, the mansion is called as "Prince Qing's Mansion".

39-40

涛贝勒府

位于柳荫街27号，原是康熙第十五子愉郡王允禑的"愉王府"。光绪二十八年(1902)，醇亲王奕譞第七子载涛过继给钟郡王奕詥为嗣，承袭贝勒爵位，迁居于愉王府，称为"涛贝勒府"。

Tao Beile's Mansion

It is located at No. 27 of Liuying Street. Originally it was "Prince Yu's Mansion" as it belonged to Yunxu, the Prefectural Monarch of Yu and the fifteenth son of Emperor Kangxi. In the twenty-eighth year of Guangxu Period (A.D. 1902), Zaitao, the seventh son of Prince Chun Yixuan, was adopted by Yiha, the Prefectural Monarch of Zhong, and became his heir. Zaitao succeeded to the Beile peerage and moved to Prince Yu's Mansion, so peple began to call this mansion "Tao Beile's Mansion".

20世纪20年代，辅仁大学在此建立，图为现存旧址。
FuRen University was established here in 1920s and the relics could still be found here.

绿树掩映下的涛贝勒府
Tao Beile's Mansion Sheltered in Greenery

错落有致的院落
Trim courtyards

棍贝子府

位于新街口东街北侧,又称诚亲王(允祉)新府。雍正十年(1732)允祉卒,其第七子弘曔继为府主。之后多易其主。光绪六年(1880)棍布札布袭贝子,此府称"棍贝子府"。

Gun Beizi's Mansion

Located north to the East Street of Xinjiekou, this mansion is also called Prince Cheng(Aisin-Gioro·Yunzhi)'s New Mansion. In the tenth year of Yongzheng Period (A.D.1732), Yunzhi died and his seventh son Hongjing succeeded and became the master of the mansion and after his death many new masters had lived there. In the sixth year of Guangxu Period (A.D.1880), Gunbuzhabu succeeded the peerage and became Beizi (rank of Manchu nobility inferior to Beile in Qing Dynasty). Since then this mansion has been called "Gun Beizi's Mansion".

盛园
位于小石桥胡同24号、后马厂胡同17号，最初是清末邮传部大臣盛宣怀的宅邸。

Shengyuan Garden
It is located at No.24 Xiaoshiqiao Hutong and No. 17 Houmachang Hutong. It used to be the residence of Sheng Huaixuan, the minister of Post and Transportation Ministry of the late Qing Dynasty.

第叁章
Chapter III

故居访名士
Visiting Former Residences of Celebrities

什刹海诸多的名人故居就像历史遗存的珍宝,为风光秀丽的什刹海凭添了浓厚的人文气息。走进静谧深幽的故居,主人生前的一草一木仍然井井有条,让我们睹物思人,回想起这些名流大家的风雨一生。

Just like treasures preserved in the history development, a great many former residences of celebrities in Shichahai area have added a touch of humanism to the beautiful sceneries. In these residences, serenity prevails and all of those belongings are still kept in order. When visiting these former residences, we can not help reminiscing over the highs and lows in the life course of these great people.

宋庆龄故居

宋庆龄（1893–1981），原籍海南文昌人，生于上海，1915年与孙中山结婚。中华人民共和国成立后历任中央人民政府副主席、国家副主席、全国人大常务委员会副委员长、国家名誉主席等职务。
故居位于后海北沿46号，原为醇亲王府花园。宋庆龄于1963年起在这里居住，直至逝世，共居住了18年。

Former Residence of Song Qingling

Song Qingling (1893-1981) was born in Shanghai and her hometown is Wenchang, Hainan Province. In 1915 she married Sun Yet-sen. After the establishment of People's Republic of China she had successively assumed the following positions: Vice President of the Central People's Government, Vice President of People's Republic of China, Vice Chairman of the Standing Committee of the National People's Congress, Honorary President of People's Republic of China. The residence is located at No. 46 of Houhai Beiyan. It used to be the Garden of Prince Chun's Mansion. Song Qingling took her residence here in 1963 and had lived here for 18 years till passed away in 1981.

瑰宝亭 Treasure Pavilion

笙亭 Fan Pavilion

长廊 Long Corridor

主楼　Main Building

郭沫若故居

郭沫若（1892-1978），四川乐山人，作家、诗人、剧作家、考古学家、古文字学家和社会活动家。故居位于前海西街18号。故居内存放着大量郭沫若的手稿以及收藏的书籍、拓片、书画、信函等。

Former Residence of Guo Moruo

Guo Moruo (1892-1978) was from Leshan, Sichuan Province. He was a writer, poet, dramatist, archaeologist, philologist of ancient writings, as well as a social activist. His former residence is located at No.18 of Qianhai Xijie, where a great many hand scripts, as well as books, rubbings, paintings, calligraphic works, correspondence, were exhibited.

院内　Inside the courtyard

书房　Writing room

郭沫若塑像 Statue of Guo Moruo

49-50

梅兰芳在《白蛇传》中饰演白素贞
Mei Lanfang plays the role of Bai Suzhen in *Madam White Snake*

梅兰芳故居
梅兰芳（1894-1961），江苏泰州人，著名京剧艺术大师。故居位于护国寺大街9号，原为庆王府的一部分。1984年成立梅兰芳研究学会，在此筹建纪念馆，1986年10月开馆。

Former Residence of Mei Lanfang
Mei Lanfang (1894-1961) was from Taizhou, Jiangsu Province. He was a master artist of Peking Opera. The residence is located at No. 9 of Huguo Temple Street and it used to be a part of Prince Qing's Mansion. In 1984, Mei Lanfang Research Society and a memorial were set up here. The memorial of Mei Lanfang opened in October, 1986.

徐悲鸿纪念馆

徐悲鸿（1895-1953），江苏宜兴人，著名画家。早年先后赴日本、法国留学。抗日期间曾以画笔从事宣传工作，解放后任中央美术学院院长。去世后家属把大量作品及收藏捐献给国家，1954年成立徐悲鸿纪念馆，拆迁后纪念馆设置在新街口北大街53号。

Memorial of Xu Beihong

Xu Beihong (1895-1953) was from Yixing, Jiangsu Province. He was a famous painter. He had studied in Japan and France when he was young. In the period of Sino-Japanese War he plunged himself into war-time propaganda with his brushes. After the liberation he became the president of China Central Academy of Fine Arts. After he passed away, his family donated a great number of his works and collections to the country. In 1954, Xu Beihong Memorial was established and later the memorial was relocated to No. 53 of Xinjiekou North Street as the former area was demolished and reconstructed.

《愚公移山》是徐悲鸿艺术顶峰时期的经典之作
How Old simpleton Removed Mountains is a classic work created by Xu Beihong in his prime days

骏马是徐悲鸿先生一生中最爱描绘的题材

Horses are Mr Xu's favorite painting object

蔡锷在京住所

蔡锷（1882–1916），原名艮寅，字松坡，湖南邵阳人。1911年响应辛亥革命武装起义，指挥云南起义。1915年12月反对袁世凯复辟帝制，起兵讨袁。其在京住所位于棉花胡同66号，他于1913年至1915年曾经在这里居住。

Former Residence of Cai Er

Cai Er (1882-1916) was from Shaoyang, Hunan Province. His old name is Gengyin and Cai Songpo is his byname. In 1911, he directed the uprise in Yunnan Province in answer to other uprises in Xinhai Revolution. In December 1915, he raised a rightous revolt against Yuan Shikai who had restored monarchy. His former residence is in No. 66 of Mianhua Hutong. He lived there from 1913 to 1915.

张之洞故居

张之洞（1837-1909），直隶南皮人，清末重臣，洋务派首领。故居位于白米斜街11号，1909年（宣统元年）张之洞病逝于此。

Former Residence of Zhang Zhidong

Zhang Zhidong (1837-1909) was from Nanpi, Zhili Province (in the present Hebei Province). He was an senior official at the end of the Qing dynasty and one of the leaders of Westernization Group. His former residence is in No. 11 of Baimixiejie Road. Zhang Zhidong died here in 1909 (the 1st year of Xuantong Period).

张伯驹故居

张伯驹（1898–1982），擅长诗词，是著名的书画家、收藏鉴赏家。曾任故宫博物院专门委员、国家文物局鉴定委员会委员、吉林省博物馆副馆长、中央文史馆馆员。故居位于后海南沿26号。

Former Residence of Zhang Boju

Zhang Boju (1898-1982) was a famous expert of Chinese poem, painter, calligrapher, collector and connoisseur. He used to be special commissioner of the Palace Museum, commissioner of the National Commission for Cultural Relics Identification under State Administration of Cultural Heritage, Vice Curator of Jilin Provincial Museum, and member of the Central Research Institute of Culture and History. His residence is in No. 26 of Houhai Nanyan.

溥杰故居

爱新觉罗·溥杰（1907–1994），宣统皇帝溥仪胞弟。故居位于护国寺街52号，是一座小型四合院。溥杰在此度过了晚年，去世后其子女将故居捐给国家。

Former Residence of Pu Jie

Aisin-Gioro Pu Jie (1907-1994) was the younger brother of Xuantong Emperor Pu Yi. His former residence is a small courtyard at No.52 of Huguo Temple Street. Pu Jie lived here during his senior years. His heirs donated the residence estate to the country after his death.

陈垣故居

陈垣（1880–1971），字援庵，广东新会人，著名的史学家和教育家。故居位于兴华胡同13号（原兴化寺街5号）。1948年陈垣搬入此处，直到去世。

Former Residence of Chen Yuan

Chen Yuan (1880-1971) alias Chen Yuan'an was born in Xinhui, Guangdong Province. He is a very famous historian and educator. His former residence is located at No.13 of Xinghua Hutong. Chen Yuan took his residence here since 1948 and lived here untill passed away.

马海德故居

马海德（1910-1988），美国人，医学博士。1933年来华，1936年参加中国工农红军，次年参加中国共产党，献身中国革命。

旧居位于后海北沿24号。1950年马海德迁居于此，直到去世。

Former Residence of Ma Haide

George Hatem is known as Ma Haide (1910-1988) who was an American and a doctor of medicine. He came to China in 1933, joined Chinese Red Army in 1936 and became a CPC member the next year. He had devoted himself to the cause of Chinese revolution. His former residence is located at No. 24 of Houhai Beiyan. Ma Haide took his residence here in 1950 and lived here till his death.

老舍故居

老舍（1899–1966），现代著名作家、杰出的语言大师，被誉为"人民艺术家"。
老舍生于小羊圈胡同（现名小杨家胡同），满族正红旗人。故居位于西城区小杨家胡同8号。

Former Residence of Lao She

Lao She (1899-1966) was a famous modern writer and master of language and was honored as "People's Artist".

Lao She was a Manchu of the Red Banner (an ethnic group in north China, the members of which are divided into eight "Banners" of different colors). He was born in Xiaoyangjuan Hutong (the present Xiaoyangjia Hutong) and his former residence is in No. 8 of Xiaoyangjia Hutong, Xicheng District.

田间故居

田间（1916-1985），著名诗人。出版了《戎冠秀》、《田间诗抄》等30余部诗集，被称为"马背诗人"。故居位于后海北沿38号，是一座小型四合院。1953年田间用稿费购得。

Former Residence of Tianjian

Tian Jian(1916-1985)was a famous poet. He is known as "poet on horseback" and had published over 30 poetry anthologies including *Rong Guanxiu, Poems of Tian Jian*. His former residence is a small courtyard located at No.38 of Houhai Beiyan. Tian Jian bought the house with remunerations from writing articles in 1953.

第肆章
Chapter IV

宝刹香火盛
Religious Sites

传说什刹海因"什刹海寺"或因环湖有众多古刹而得名。
什刹海寺庙的历史可追溯到隋、唐时期。历代或敕封、或募建、或私立，先后建有各类寺院、道观、教堂、祠堂、家庙等宗教场所百余座。

Legends hold that it is either from a temple called Shichahai Temple or because there are many ancient temples surrounding the lake that the name of Shichahai origins.

The history of the temples of Shichahai district could be traced back to Sui-Tang Period. In the past centuries, various religious sites have been built here with funds from the government or private donators. In this area, you can find Buddhist and Taoist temples, churches, ancestral halls, family temples, etc and the total number amounts to one hundred plus.

关岳庙

位于鼓楼西大街149号,国家级文物保护单位。原为醇亲王奕譞庙,1914年北洋政府塑关羽、岳飞像,并祀称关岳庙。

Guan-Yue Temple

It is located at No. 149 of Gulou West Street. It used to be temple devoted to Yixuan, Prince Chun and in 1914 the Northern Warlords Government built sculptures of ancient general Guan Yu and Yue Fei and started offering sacrifices to them. It was from then on that this temple has become Guan-Yue Temple. It is now a state level cultural relic preservation unit.

鼓楼　Drum Tower

祈福　Praying for happiness and blessing

广化寺

位于后海鸦儿胡同31号，始建于元代，明清时期曾重修。清宣统元年（1909）曾在寺内筹建京师图书馆。1939年在寺内创办广化佛学院。现为北京市佛教协会所在地。

Guanghua Temple

It is located at No.31 of Houhai Ya'er Hutong. The construction started in Yuan Dynasty and reconstruction had been done successively in Ming and Qing dynasties. In the first year of Xuantong Period in Qing Dynasty (A.D. 1909), the authority planned to build Capital Library inside the temple. In 1939, Guanghua Buddhist School was founded in the temple. Now the Buddhist Association of Beijing locates in this temple.

佛门宝刹，万法庄严。
Impressive gate leads to majestic Buddhist temple where Buddhist power is immense.

火德真君庙

"火德真君"为道教司火之神。庙宇位于地安门外大街77号,俗称"火神庙"。据传为唐贞观年间(627–649)所建。元至正六年(1346)重修。明万历三十三年(1605)重建。

Temple of the God of Fire

The temple, known as the "Temple of Fire God", is located at No.77 of Di'anmen Wai Street. The temple was constructed in Tang Dynasty and first rebuilt in Yuan Dynasty and then reconstructed again in Ming Dynasty.

往事如烟
The past disappears like mist.

护国寺
位于护国寺街85号，北京市文物保护单位。寺庙始建于元代，坐北朝南，规模宏大，现存金刚殿。

Huguo Temple
It was located at No. 85 of Huguo Temple Street and is a Municipal Level Cultural Relic Protection Unit. The temple was first built in Yuan Dynasty and its front faces south. The temple had been magnigicent but now only the Hall of Buddha's Warrior Attendants remains.

金刚殿
The Hall of Buddha's Warrior Attendants

大藏龙华寺

位于后海北沿23号。建于明成化三年（1467），清康熙五十八年（1719）重建。清道光年间曾改名"心华寺"，为拈花寺的下院，后为清醇亲王府载沣祠堂。

Dazang Longhua Temple

It is located at No. 23 of Houhai Beiyan. The temple was built in the third year of Chenghua Period in Ming Dynasty (A.D.1467) and reconstructed in the fifty-eighth year of Kangxi Period in Qing Dynasty. In Daoguang Period of Qing Dynasty, its name was once changed to "Xinhua Temple" and the temple itself became the subordinate temple of Nianhua Temple and later the sacrifice memorial of Zaifeng, Prince Chun of Qing royal family.

贤良祠

贤良祠位于地安门西大街103号旁门。建于清雍正八年（1730），是祭祀国家功臣的地方。门额上有雍正皇帝御书"崇忠念旧"。

Memorial Temple of Eminent Statesmen

Memorial of Talented and Virtuous Figures is located at the Side Gate of No. 103 Di'anmen West Street. It was constructed in the eighth year of Yongzheng Period in Qing Dynasty (A.D. 1730) as a place to offer sacrifices to country heroes in the past. On the door head, Emperor Yongzheng had left his handwritten inscription which reads "chongzhongnianjiu", means to advocate the sense of loyalty and to memorialize the late eminent statesmen.

藻井 Caisson Ceiling

大门 Front Gate

第伍章
Chapter V

古桥倚夕阳
Ancient Bridges in Sunset

什刹海地区水域狭长，大小桥梁点缀其中。无论是久已远去的三座桥、西步粮桥，还是至今仍然承载着南北交通的万宁桥、银锭桥、德胜桥，都记载着京城的历史变迁。

The waters of Shichahai area are mostly in very narrow and long shape. Bridges of various sizes dot along these water courses. Today, Sanzuo Bridge and Xiliang Bridge are no longer in existence but Wanning Bridge, Yinding Bridge and Desheng Bridge are still in function. All of them have witnessed the historical changes in the capital city.

万宁桥
位于北京城中轴线北段,地安门外大街中部。始建于元代,曾是通惠河的重要枢纽。

Wanning Bridge
Situated at the north part of central axle and in the central part of Di`anmen Wai street. It was first built in Yuan Dynasty and had served as an important terminal of Tonghui Canal.

银锭桥
位于前海与后海交接处。始建于明代，是北京著名景点之一。

Yinding Bridge
Situated at the joint point of Qianhai Lake and Houhai Lake. It was first constructed in Ming Dynasty. Enjoying the great view of Xishang mountain from Yinding Bridge has been one of the famous sights of Beijing.

德胜桥

位于后海与西海连接处,始建于明代。

Desheng Bridge

It was located at the joint point of Houhai and Xihai. The construction started in Ming Dynasty.

京味民风
Hunting for Typical Beijing Features

俗话说"先有什刹海，后有北京城"。一条条胡同，曲曲折折；一声声京腔，韵味悠长。什刹海的每个角落，都透着浓浓的北京味儿。老北京的味儿，藏在海子波光闪闪的韵致里，藏在青砖灰瓦的街巷里，藏在鸟笼棋局间的随意里。临水而居的人们，闲适、雅致，充满生活情调。

As the saying goes "Beijing City was born after Shichahai area came into being". There are typical Beijing features hidden in every corner of Shichahai area, in the grace of the lake shimmering with ripples, in the Hutongs built of grey bricks and tiles, and in the pleasure of birds raising and chess playing. Residents in this area lead an easy life that is full of fun.

肆	叁	贰	壹
缤纷手工艺 Colorful Handicrafts	百姓享盛世 Daily Life in a Prosperous Age	美食风味浓 Gourmand's Delight	胡同意味长 Hutongs and Their Stories

第壹章
Chapter I

胡同意味长
Hutongs and Their Stories

北京的胡同原本就是一道景观，而什刹海的胡同更是别具一格。胡同两侧的四合院错落有序，与周边景致浑然天成。

Hutong in itself is a typical sight of Beijing. Hutongs in Shichahai area has their own charisteristics. Courtyard complexes on both sides of the Hutong are of trim layout and in great harmony with the surrounding environment.

老墙，爬山虎，昔日的老屋。
Old wall, ivy and the old house

如意门
Wish gratification gate

什刹海是个令人怀旧的地方。长长的小巷里，蕴藏着久已尘封的故事。
Shichahai is a place full of memories. There are stories behind every long lane.

瓦檐滴水
Water dripping from the eave

古树成行
Age-old trees lining in row

79-80

"百花深处"留下许多情
"Baihuashengchu (means deep in the flowering shrubs) Hutong" has witnessed many stories

糖房大院
Grand Yard of Sugar Workshops

龙头井胡同　Longtoujing Hutong

南官房胡同　Nanguanfang Hutong

老北京民居既有北方民居的朴拙大方，又有江南民居的雅致。工匠常常把他们的艺术匠心倾注在一扇窗子、一块石雕上。

The old residences of Beijing folks have integrated both the simplicity of the northern architectures and the elegance of the southern buildings. Every window sill and stone carving exhibit the high technique of the craftsmen.

"天棚鱼缸石榴树,先生肥狗胖丫头"。如意门、影壁、正房、东西厢房、倒座房、耳房、后罩房……讲究的院落布置,严整的建筑格局,使四合院成为什刹海文化不可或缺的一部分。

"Sunshade, fish tank, and megranate trees; teachers, fat dog and plump maids" used to be indispensable elements of a courtyard. Courtyards in Shichahai area are usually in elaborate design and in neat formation with components such as the wish-gratifying gate, screen walls opposite the main door, central rooms, wing rooms on both sides, the opposite room facing northward, penthouses, the row of rooms behind the central rooms, and etc. Courtyard has been an indispensible element of Shichahai culture.

繁花满园
A glimpse through blossom

书香门第
Inside a scholar's house

四合院的宜居生活
Nice environment inside a courtyard

庭院深深深几许。穿过月亮门,进入四合院,墙外的市井之声渐行渐远。

Courtyards in Shichahai area enjoy great serenity. Passing through the moon-shaped gate, you are in a courtyard and the bustling of the world dies away.

第贰章
Chapter II

百姓享盛世
Daily Life in a Prosperous Age

一方水土养一方人，生活在什刹海的人们不仅民风淳朴，更有"卜居积水，世守砚田"的情致。置身什刹海，不仅能体验到原汁原味的老北京文化，更能感受到老北京人和睦相处、安居乐业的宽广心态。

Residents in Shichahai area are not only simple and honest in nature but always in pursuit of culture and art accomplishment. Touring Shichahai, you can not only experience the essence of Beijing folk culture but can also sense the peaceful mindset of the local people.

住了几十年的老人
Senior residents who have lived here for dozens of years

午后下盘棋
Playing chess in the afternoon

雨中遇到老街坊
Having a chat in the rain

若无闲事挂心头,便是人间好时节。小胡同的居民在宁静的四合院里安享太平,日子虽然平静,却也充满情趣,家长里短,柴米油盐,也有滋有味。

Care-free days are most precious. The residents in the narrow Hutongs enjoy peaceful days inside the courtyards. Days running on smoothly and common daily life is full of fun.

金玉满堂
Enjoy leisure hours

中元放荷灯
Floating Lotus Lights on the evening of Chinese Ghost Festival (in the middle of lunar July)

端午赛龙舟
Dragon boats contests in Dragon Festival

欢庆锣鼓
Gongs and drums performance

传承什刹海,自有后来人。
Younger generation is the hope of Shichahai.

第叁章
Chapter III

美食风味浓
Gourmand's Delight

来到什刹海,不仅可以大饱眼福,更可让你大饱口福!烤肉季、全聚德、护国寺小吃、九门小吃……数目众多的特色美食,不要说是亲口尝尝,就是想想都会心动神往。

When touring Shichahai, you can satisfy your eyes and stomach at the same time. Kaorou Ji, Quanjude, snacks offered by Huguosi snack counters and by Jiumen Snack Shop…there are numerous choices! You could hardly resist the temptation of so many delicacies.

烤肉季　Kaorou Ji

全聚德　Quanjude

九门小吃
汇集了包括小肠陈、爆肚冯、茶汤李、年糕钱、奶酪魏、豆腐脑白等传统小吃。

Jiumen Snack Shop
Snacks you can get from Jiumen Snack Shop: " Small Intestine Chen", "Saute Stomach Feng", "Sweet Soup Lee", "Rice Cake Qian", "Cheese Wei" and "Doufu Flower Bai" , and etc.

护国寺小吃

经营艾窝窝、豌豆黄、切糕、豆面糕、糖火烧、豆汁、焦圈等几十种小吃,深受大众欢迎。

Snacks offered by Huguosi snack counters

Snacks you can get from Huguosi snack counters: Aiwowo (a steamed cone-shaped cake made of glutinous rice or millet with a sweet filling), Wandouhuan (pea-flour cakes), Qiegao (Sticky rice cake slices), Doumiangao (glutinous rice rolls with sweetened bean flour coating), Tanghuoshao (baked cake with brown sugar and sesame paste), Jiaoquan (crisply fried ring of dough) and etc.

第肆章
Chapter IV

缤纷手工艺
Colorful Handicrafts

什刹海历来就是民间手工艺活动聚集之地，无论是泥塑彩绘、风筝扎制、山核桃粘贴，还是鬃人、毛猴、皮影、鼻烟壶内画，都反映了老北京民间文化的传承与发展。

Shichahai used to be the venue for folk handicrafts. These handicrafts, including color-painted clay sculptures, kite making, hickory stickups, bristle figures, monkey dolls, shadow play pieces, snuff bottle inner wall painting, and etc, have all reflected the inheritance and development trends of Beijing folk art.

泥塑彩绘民间艺人双起翔
Shuang Qixiang, folk art craftsman of painted-clay-figure making

鬃人民间艺人白大成
Bai Dacheng, folk art craftsman of bristle-figure making

风筝民间艺人刘宾
Liu B n, folk art craftsman of kite-making

山核桃粘贴民间艺人丁月华
Ding Yuehua, folk art craftsman of hickory-stickup making

什刹海为许多民间手工艺人提供了取之不尽的艺术创作灵感。

Shichahai is the fountain of inspirations for many folk art artists.

鼻烟壶内画民间艺人李静
Li Jing, folk art craft-woman of snuff-bottle-inner-wall painting

皮影民间艺人路连达
Lu Lianda, folk artist of shadow-play performing

风筝民间艺人王赤峰
Wang Chifeng, folk art craftsman of kite-making

年近百岁的剪纸民间艺人葛秉华
Ge Binghua, folk art craft-woman of paper-cutting who is about a hundred years old

毛猴民间艺人任文仲
Ren Wenzhong, folk art craftsman of monkey-doll making

悦

新装多姿
Face-Lift for More Fun

新中国成立后，什刹海发生了翻天覆地的变化。火神庙修复告捷，银锭桥春色醉人，野鸭岛生机盎然……所有的一切，都在讴歌和谐的乐章。

什刹海的今天，人与景，古与今，时尚与传统，就如同朝晖与夕阳一样和谐共存。这种和谐，将在每一个什刹海人手中发扬光大，世代流传。

After the establishment of the People's Republic of China, Shichahai experienced great changes. Repairs and renovations have been done here.

Today in Shichahai, environment-friendly measures have been taken and everything is in great harmony which embodies human and nature, ancient elements and contemporary elements, traditional elements and trendy elements. This harmony will be cherished and intensified by everyone living and working in Shichahai area and passed on from generation to generation.

肆 叁 贰 壹
保护与传承 旧迹换新颜 休闲新风尚 旅游事业兴
Preservation and Cultural... Renovation Efforts Leisure Trends Booming Tourist Industry...

第壹章
Chapter I

旅游事业兴
Booming Tourist Industry

什刹海的美会让亲历过的人牵挂一生。

什刹海水域宽阔，旅游资源丰富。坐上橹船，信桨泛舟，伴着悠悠古曲，尽赏岸边美景，任由清风徐来……

收起船桨，漫步垂柳岸堤、胡同民居，浓郁的老北京风情迎面而来。

You will never forget Shichahai once you have witnessed her beauty.

There are large water areas in Shichahai and the tourist resources are abundant. You can rent a boat and scull at leisure in the gentle breeze with traditional Chinese folk music in the background while enjoying attractive sceneries along the bank.

You can also stroll along the bank lined with willows or loiter into the depth of the Hutong, hunting for typical Beijing features.

胡同游

胡同是老北京文化的鲜活载体，随着世人对胡同文化的日益关注，"胡同游"应运而生。游客乘坐人力三轮车，在什刹海风景区的大小胡同中穿行，融入老北京的日常生活中。

Tours through Hutong

Hutong is the live carrier of Beijing's age-old culture. As people pay more and more attention to the culture of Hutong, Hutong touring booms to meet the rising demand. Tourists can take pedicabs and travel through Hutongs of various sizes inside the scenic zone of Shichahai and have a close look at the daily lives of Beijing old timers.

外国友人对胡同文化情有独衷
Foreign friends have special interest in Hutong culture

老胡同里寻风问俗
Local customs hunting in ancient Hutong

走进什刹海，逛逛老北京。
Strolling in Shichahai area and gaining more knowledge about age-old Beijing city

游人对屋檐下的鸟充满好奇
Tourists are fascinated by the birds

信手一曲《出水莲》
The familiar tune of *Lotus Flower out of Water* is at the players' fingertips.

水上游
什刹海的湖光水色引人入胜,"水上游"很受游客欢迎。人们乘着橹船,听古乐、品香茗、赏美景。倘若兴致盎然,还可以体验月夜放河灯的乐趣。

On-water Tourism
The waterscape of Shichahai is especially attractive and the on-water tours are very popular. Tourists can take sculling boats to enjoy the beautiful sceneries while appreciating traditional Chinese folk music and savouring fragrant tea. If you are in high spirit, you may have a try at delivering floating lights on the lake in moonlit nights.

误入藕花深处
Way into the depth of lotus flower clusters

第贰章
Chapter II

休闲新风尚
Leisure Trends

随着社会的发展，古朴的什刹海也融入了众多时尚元素，酒吧、茶座、咖啡馆，受到时尚休闲一族的青睐。
夜晚的什刹海更是霓虹闪烁，游人如织。徜徉在这里，您可以领略多元文化融合带来的视觉盛宴。

With the development of the society, many trendy elements have found their way into age-old Shichahai area. Bars and cafes here have attracted lots of trendy people.

In the evening, Shichahai is splendid with neon lights on. It's here that you can enjoy a visual feast abundant in diverse culture elements.

茶艺酒吧街

什刹海风景区美仑美奂的景致，吸引着中外游客纷至沓来，带动了这一地区茶艺、酒吧的兴起，使什刹海茶艺酒吧街享誉京城。

Tea Shop and Tavern Street

The enchanting sceneries of Shichahai scenic zone have attracted tourists from home and abroad and boosted the business of tea shops and pubs. The Tea Shop and Tavern Street of Shichahai is now a renowned place in the city.

人们用各种各样的方式感受什刹海的休闲氛围。

People enjoy their leisure hours in Shichahai in various ways.

特色小店

文化味浓厚的小店,吸引了很多游客参观选购。这些小店的商品,大都崇尚手工、信仰自然,一件件都个性十足,鲜有工业时代的呆板与复制。

Unique Shops

Shops rich in cultural features attract many tourists. The commodities sold in these shops are mostly handicrafts of unique designs and full of individuality. In these shops, you will never be bored by dullness and replication.

第叁章
Chapter III
旧迹换新颜
Renovation Efforts

初次走进什刹海的人，都会被这里的优美环境所折服。无论街衢民巷，还是广场小园，一切都是整洁有序，独具匠心。经过多年的精心治理，如今什刹海风光如洗，景色宜人，成为名副其实的首善之地。

时间在变，景色在变，唯一不变的是什刹海人对这方水土的深深眷恋。

If it's your first-time tour in Shichahai, you will be impressed by beautiful environment here. From alleys, streets to gardens, everywhere is tidy and in order. After years of renovation, Shichahai has restored its original feature and beautiful sceneries. It has really become the model district of the whole country.

Time flies and sceneries change. The only thing that remains unchanged is the affection Shichahai people bear toward this land.

野鸭 Wild Ducks

野鸭岛 Wild Duck Island

野鸭岛是什刹海生态环境转变的最好见证，不仅野鸭愿意留下来，时时还会有斑头雁、大雁、鸳鸯等野生鸟类在此停留。或许，它们和人们一样，深深留恋着这里的碧水蓝天。

Wild Duck Island is the best proof of the ecological improvement of the local environment. Not only wild ducks take residence here happily, wild fowls, such as bar-headed gooses, common large gooses, mandarin ducks, and etc. , all take rest here quite often. Maybe they are also in love with beautiful sceneries here as human beings do.

夜鷺 Night Heron

什刹海地区随处可见的文化休闲广场是居民休憩的乐园。人们在这里打太极、唱京戏、抖空竹、放风筝，展示什刹海人的精神风尚。

In Shichahai area, squares for culture and leisure activities can be seen everywhere. They have become venues for local residents to play Taiji, practise Peking opera, play diabolos and fly kites. It's at these venues that the spiritual outlook of Shichahai people is demonstrated.

综合治理后的街区，焕然一新、整洁有序。

Streets and residential areas are tidy and in order after comprehensive renovation.

德胜门内大街
Deshengmen Nei Street

护国寺大街
Huguosi Street

在街区整治过程中,一些老街的古朴韵味得到充分保护。著名的烟袋斜街经过系统改造后,店铺林立,商业繁荣。

During the process of renovation, the old features of some old streets have been well preserved. After a systematic renovation, the famous YandaiXieJie Street has witnessed a great boom in business.

改造后的后海南沿
Houhai Nanyan after renovation

第肆章
Chapter IV

保护与传承
Preservation and Inheritance

改革开放三十年，什刹海历史文化的保护与传承得到前所未有的重视。在保护与利用、整治与发展方面，取得了可喜的成果。恭王府、火神庙、广福观……一大批珍贵遗产得到全面修复，几百年的古风神韵在今朝重现。

In the past thirty years, under the guidance of opening-up and reform policy, unprecedented attention has been given to the historical and cultural heritages in Shichahai area. Great achievements have been attained in respect to preservation, utilization, renovation and development. A great number of precious heritage including Prince Gong's Mansion, Fire God's Temple, Guangfu Taoist Temple, and etc. have all been repaired comprehensively. Ancient features and magnificence can again be observed nowadays.

广福观始建于明代天顺年间，2008年开始全面修复。
Guangfu Taoist Temple was first constructed in Tianshun Period of Ming Dynasty and it is in 2008 that the overall renovation has been done.

恭王府修复功告大成，工作人员挂上喜庆的红灯笼。

The renovation of Prince Gong's Mansion has been completed and staff members are putting up red lanterns for celebration.

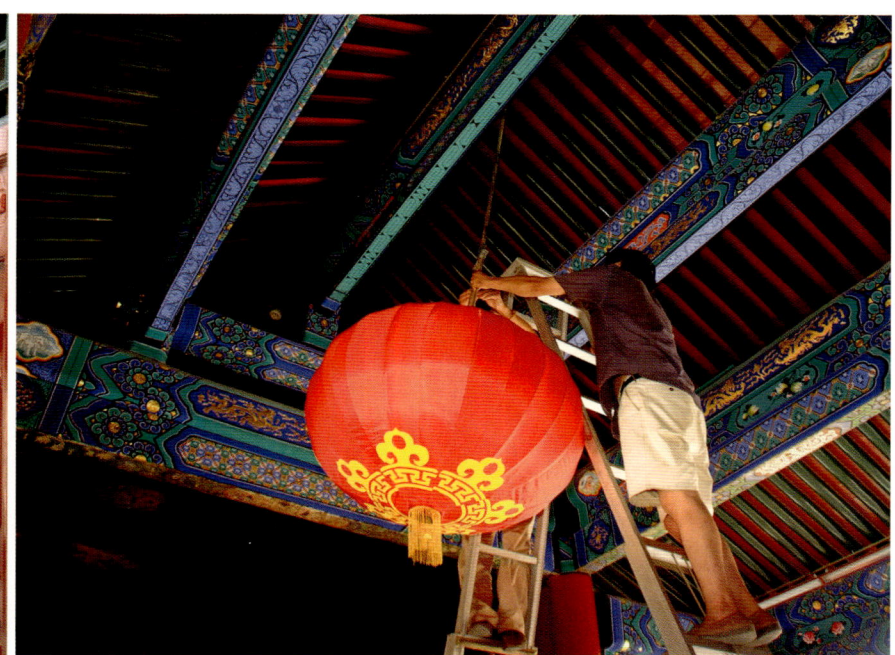

汇通祠始建于明代永乐年间，重新规划建设后，以崭新的面貌呈现在世人面前。现辟为郭守敬纪念馆。

Huitong Temple was first constructed in Yongle Period of Ming Dynasty. After reconstruction, the temple is in brand new condition and seats Guoshoujing Memorial.

后　记

什刹海是一部史书，它镌刻着元、明、清三朝古都的岁月印迹；什刹海是一幅画卷，它展现了"西湖春、秦淮夏、洞庭秋"的秀美与壮阔；什刹海是北京城的一张名片，名片上印着老北京的闲适与现代都市的时尚。如今的什刹海，每天游人如织，来自世界各地、有着不同肤色、操着不同语言的游客，到这里寻找属于自己的梦。我们编辑出版这本画册，就是要把这里的文化底蕴、这里的秀丽风光通过图片展示出来，奉献给读者，让来自四面八方的人们感受什刹海的永久魅力。

本书的出版，得到了社会各界的鼎力支持。在图片拍摄搜集过程中，广大居民、游客和相关景点管理部门全力配合，并提供了许多珍贵历史图片；在文字编纂之际，许多专家学者不辞辛劳，献计献策。在此我们表示诚挚感谢。由于什刹海文化涉及面很广，书中难免有疏漏之处，希望大家批评指正。

Postscript

Shichahai is a book of history which marks the traces of the capital as it witnessed highs and lows of Yuan, Ming and Qing dynasties over hundreds of years. Shichahai is also a great painting which embodys both quaintness and magnificence as it is compared as "West Lake in spring, Qinhuai River in summer and Dongting Lake in autumn." Shichahai is a showcase of Beijing, where easy lifestyle of old-time Beijing and trends of modern city are exhibited. Nowadays, numerous tourists, who are from different corners of the world and of different nationalities, visit Shichahai area every day in pursuit of their own dreams. We present this album with the attempt to demonstrate the charm of local culture and the beautiful sceneries as well. We also hope that from this album, you can sense the everlasting glamour of Shichahai that embodies various culture elements.

This album is published with kind supports from various social circles and communities. A great many local residents, tourists and authorities have offered their help. When compiling the text, many experts and scholars have contributed their valuable suggestions and opinions. We would like to extend our gratitude towards all these people here. Comments and suggestions are warmly welcome.

书　　　名：中国最美的城区之一——北京什刹海

顾　　　问：杨胜博　李思平

主　　　编：傅　华

副　主　编：王国建　徐　斌

执行副主编：唐景平　高建军

编　　　委：包旭东　王恩柱　聂殿维　冯卯辰　张艳芳　陈　杨　徐　文　张亚群　张伟生

摄　　　影：王燕京　温宝华　陈延宏　朱振立　张　胜　赵志刚　潘惠涛　时安源　闫玉成　董友烺　甄洪绵　刁立生

编著单位：中共北京市西城区委什刹海街道工作委员会

　　　　　　北京市西城区人民政府什刹海街道办事处

图书再版编目（CIP）数据

中国最美的城区之一 ——北京什刹海／北京市西城区什刹海街道工委、办事处 编著. —北京：当代中国出版社，2008.9
  ISBN 978-7-80170-757-4
  Ⅰ.中… Ⅱ.北… Ⅲ.名胜古迹–西城区–画册 Ⅳ.K 928.701.3-64

中国版本图书馆CIP数据核字（2008）第143567号

出 版 人：周五一
责任编辑：陈立旭
英文编辑：叶秀敏
英文翻译：叶秀敏　任小平
设　　计：北京恒瑞盛世设计有限公司　http://www.z-hrss.com
印　　刷：北京画中画印刷有限公司　http://www.pip-print.cnz-hrss.com
开　　本：大12开
印　　张：12
版　　次：2008年9月第1版
印　　次：2008年9月第1次印刷
定　　价：298.00元

版权所有，翻版必究；如有印装质量问题，请与出版部联系（010）66572159

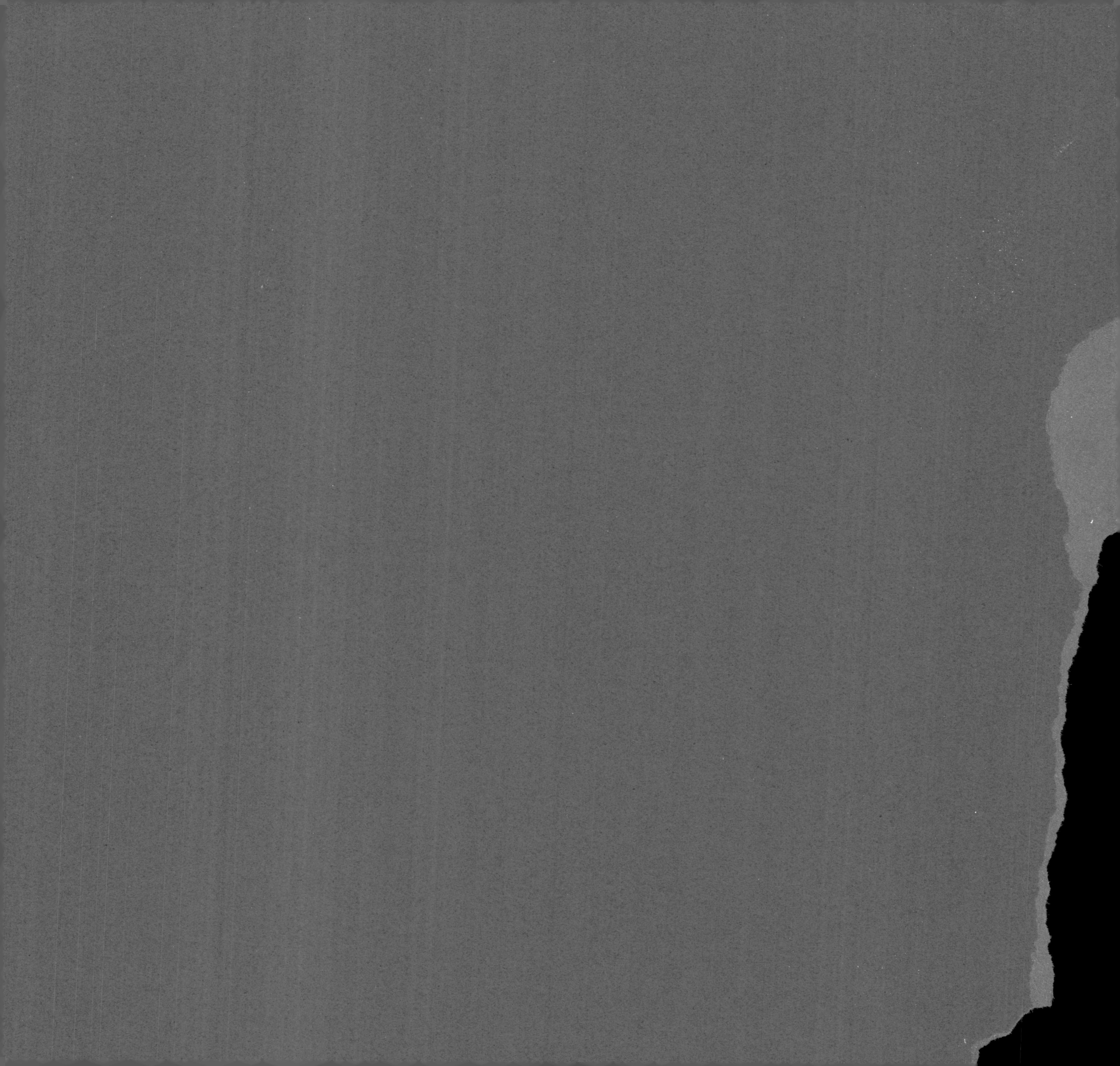